Esther von Krosigk
Pope Francis

Esther von Krosigk

Pope Francis

Interesting, amusing and moving
anecdotes about the Pontifax
from South America

Translation from the German by
John Legg

Fromm Verlag

Imprint
Bibliographic information published by the Deutsche
Nationalbibliothek: The Deutsche Nationalbibliothek
lists this publication in the Deutsche Nationalbiblio-
grafie; detailed bibliographic data are available in the
Internet at http://dnb.dnb.de.

Translation from the German
by John Legg

Cover photo by arrangement with L'Osservatore
Romano, Vatikan.

Publishing House
Fromm Verlag is an imprint of AV Akademikerverlag
GmbH & Co. KG, Heinrich-Böcking-Str. 6-8, 66121
Saarbrücken, Germany

www.frommverlag.de

Printed in Germany Books on Demand GmbH,
D-22848 Norderstedt

ISBN
978-3-639-83612-7

Content

Childhood and Youth

Jorge Mario Bergoglio spent his childhood with his parents and four siblings in Flores, a district of Buenos Aires. They led the modest life of an immigrant family in the bourgoise quarter, dominated by plane trees, of the Argentine capital. His father José Mario Francisco Bergoglio had emigrated from Portacomaro near Asti in the Italien Piedmont to Argentina and had found a job on the railways. In 1935 he married the native Argentine Regina Maria Sivori whose forefathers came from Italy too. Jorge Mario was their first child, Alberto Horacio, Oscar Adrian, Marta Regina and Maria Elena followed. At home the family spoke the soft, melodic Spanish of the Rio de la Plata and, of course, Italian, the language of their forefathers.

◇

The Pope has never forgotten his roots - he still masters the Piedmont dialect as well as the songs of the immigrants.

◇

He was born on the 17th of December 1936, the remembrance day of the Holy Sturmi, a missionary from Bavaria who, as a Bonifacius student and founder and first abbot of the Fulda monastery, played an important role in the christianisation of the Saxons. It's interesting to note that Bergoglio's birthday coincides with the Remembrance Day of a Bavarian since 76 years later Jorge Mario Bergoglio succeeded Pope Benedict XVI, also a Bavarian who additionally, as a young man, was ordained as priest in the cathedral of Freising and who taught at the high school there. Freising and its surroundings is the home of Holy Sturmi.

◇

The small house in the Calle Membrillar 531 where Bergoglio grew up was flat-roofed and single-storied. In the mean time, many floors have been added and it has been modernised - not exactly to its advantage. It has a dark brown clinker facade and a protruding balcony on the top floor. But the steps, the railings, the small terrace and the inside courtyard have remained. Jorge played here with his sisters, played football and got his knees cut. The present owner of the house, Arturo Blanco, conducts the international press with pride and zeal through the house and answers all questions although he doesn't know the Pope personally. Presumably he doesn't yet realise what it means to own and manage a future place of pilgrimage.

◇

In November 2012 Cardinal Bergoglio gave a very private interview to the local radio station 'La 96, Voz de Caacupé' in the Barracas quarter of Buenos Aires in which he spoke about his childhood. His nearest brother was only 13 months younger than he, which meant that his mother was completely overtaxed with the two small children. So Jorge was sent to his grandmother during the day whose influence on him then and also later proved to be considerable. She taught the little boy how to pray and read him stories from the Bible. In his young years Jorge Bergoglio had learned the Piedmont language and only later Spanish.

◇

The following fateful occurrence of the emigration of the Bergoglios to Argentina at the end of 1920s makes the rounds. Long before the planned departure in 1927, the family had bought their tickets for the passenger ship "Principessa Mafalda". The crossing was to take fourteen days from Genoa via Rio de Janeiro to Buenos Aires. But the Bergoglios had problems selling their household in Italy, they made no or little progress. For better or for worse they had to cancel their passage and delay their departure by a few months. This was their good fortune since the "Principessa Mafalda" sank in October 1927 off the Brasilian coast. Hundreds of people died. It was one of the biggest tragedies in the Italian shipping industry. The Bergoglios eventually arrived in Argentinia in 1929, seven years before the present Pope was born.

◊

Jorge Mario Bergoglio's sister María Elena told reporters once that their father often said that "the advent of fascism was the reason that really pushed him to leave Italy".

◊

The Pope still has the Argentinian and Italian nationalities which of course made his start with the patriotic Italians much easier.

◇

Jorge Mario Bergoglio received his first communion in the church of Divine Mercy very near his parent's home. It was a very happy ceremony attended by his parents and grandparents. At that time the idea of becoming a priest was only one of many. Bergoglio could have imagined becoming a doctor, engineer or musician, ideas typical for a boy of his age.

◇

Jorge Mario Bergoglio has been an avid football fan since childhood. He played passionately and, although only nine, sat alone in the stands and followed every home match of his beloved team San Lorenzo de Almagro where his father also played basketball.

◇

The club won the championship in 1946 and Jorge experienced this at close range. He was totally enraptured by all this - the atmosphere in the stadium, the cheering and shouting of the crowd and by the rejoicing of every goal. Deeply impressed, he still mentions this day in his sermons. Even today, 60 years later, he can recite the names of that 1950 team. He is club member number 88235 at San Lorenzo.

As Archbishop and Cardinal he celebrated a mass in 2008 for the 100th anniversary of the famous club. The players presented the famous clergyman a blue and red club shirt signed with all their names. Since his proclamation to Pope he is called 'The First Raven Pope'. The fans of San Lorenzo answer to the name of The Ravens.

◇

School friends report that Jorge Mario was a quiet and industrious student who never argued with others nor fought them. And that he always gave some of his sandwiches to his classmates - even then he was willing to share.

◇

Yes, and their were ladies in the earlier, worldly life of the present Pope... Amalia Damonte lived near Jorge Mario Bergoglio, they used to play with each other and when they were twelve they fell in love. In a very romantic letter, the present Pope asked for the hand of the girl and even painted a picture of the house in which he wanted to live together with her after their marriage. Amalia said in a TV interview in March 2013 that she was probably the reason why the young Bergoglio finally decided to lead a religious life. He had told her quite clearly that he would become a priest if she refused his proposal of marriage. In fact she was forced to do so since her parents were strongly against Bergoglio. Not only that - her mother tore the letter into pieces and her father gave her a strict talking to. Exactly ten years later Bergoglio entered the Argentine priest seminary for the first time, whilst Amalia married another man and had children.

She has never spoken to Jorge since.

Even as a young seminarian, he "was dazzled by a girl I met at an uncle's wedding", so much so that he "could not pray for over a week" because he could not help thinking of her, and so he "had to rethink what I was doing".

◇

In his first days as Pope, St. Francis mentioned Satan many times in sermons and speeches - apparently he himself had been something of a devil as a child, wild and a head full of silly ideas. The nun Marta Rabino remembers that he was extremely lively and a little devil "as every boy is". Sister Rosa who taught him was of a similar opinion. As an adult, the present Pope insisted on hearing these stories from his teacher again and again. At the end of these reminiscences she always asked the same question: "Have you improved since then?" To which Bergoglio apparently replied with a mischievous smile.

◇

His parents sent their slim and very tall son to a higher school where, just turned twenty, he served an apprenticeship as chemical technician and worked for a few years in that capacity in the foods section at Hickethier-Bachmann Laboratory. But school friends tell us that he had already decided at that time that he would become a priest.

◇

When he was twenty-one he suffered from life-threatening pneumonia and three cysts were discovered in Jorge Mario's lungs, part of his right lung was removed. After the operation he hung between life and death - which could have strengthened his decision to become a priest. Since then the Holy Father lives a very disciplined life taking care to always speak quietly and slowly. His movements too are leisurely but he - apart from sciatica which troubles him again and again - enjoys good health. And he proved that he is able to stand up to pressure as his long time as leader of the Diocese of Buenos Aires showed.

◇

Bergoglio's spirituality is based on practical brotherly love and prayer. His maxim was always: doing and action must always tally. "Only when thinking, feeling and doing are equal can it be good." Jorge Mario Bergoglio always went out on the the streets and into the poorest quarters to reach the people with belief and faith. He conveys a simple and undemanding form of piety which quickly made him very popular and will contribute to his popularity as Pope.

◇

The adolescent Jorge Mario Bergoglio often considered becoming a priest. But during his apprenticeship as chemical technician he experienced a situation which decided for him once and for all that he would do so: On a 21st of September in the middle of the 1950's he was passing with friends the Basilica San José in the Flores Quarter of Buenos Aires. The neo-baroque church with its figures of the Holy Joseph and a replica of the Virgin of Lujan at the entrance lies only two streets away from the house where Bergoglio grew up.
Bergoglio told his friends that he just wanted to take a look inside the church. But as he

entered, he immediately noticed an unknown priest taking his seat in the confessional. When Bergoglio talks about this he admits that he didn't really know what happened to him at that moment, "I felt that someone just drew me into the confessional." At the end of his confession he knew definitely that he had to become a priest.

Some time later he learned that his confessional priest, who came from the province of Corrientes in the north-east of the country, was at that time suffering from an incurable illness and died a year later of cancer.

◇

After this, Bergoglio did everything to fullfil his vocation and his mission. He studied humanities in Chile and after returning to Buenos Aires began his theology and philosophy studies at the Máximo San José College in San Miguel. During this time he was strongly influenced by his teacher Lucio Gera, a well known Argentine theologian. In December 1969, then 33, Bergoglio was consecrated priest by the Archbishop Ramon Jose Castellano. Four years later he began his six year period as Provincial of the Jesuites. So a late start was followed by a 'blitz' career.

◇

Francis is an early bird. He begins his day with intensive prayer, mostly between 4 am and 7 am each morning. In order to maintain this disciplined time of prayer he goes to bed early. You hardly ever see him at a sociable gathering late in the evening.

◇

He is considered a moderate and concilliant theologian. Conservatives value his role with the Jesuits and Liberals his support for the Church in developing countries. Bergoglio is very close to the conservative and socially engaged movement 'Communione e Liberazione'. He is for sure not the shrewd intellectual his predecessor Benedict XVI was. Bergoglio is well read with his feet firmly on the ground and with an infectious cordiality which led him to the Favelas and out to the people. He seldom seeks centre stage but when he does he always has something worthwhile to say. The effects of globalisation and the deep cleft between rich and poor are amongst his special subjects. "The uneven distribution of wealth and goods is a disgraceful injustice and robs many brothers and sisters of the opportunity to lead a full life" was his main topic at a meeting of Latin American bishops in 2007.

In his first sermon after the Conclave the new Pope concentrated on the, for him, most important subjects and figures: these are the Holy Ghost, Virgin Mary and the Devil. In connection with the last named he quoted the French author Léon Bloy who died in 1917: "He who doesn't pray to the Lord prays to the Devil." And with this quotation Bergoglio expressed his own deep conviction: He who does not confess his belief in Jesus Christ by Christian behaviour automatically confesses to the other side - to Satan, to Evil.

◇

In further sermons and speeches the new Pope swore to love, compassion and, yes, even to tenderness. He reminded us that true power lies not in the material but in the love of one's fellow men and in the service to the community. This naturally also applies to the institution Church which should be a 'poor church for the poor'.

◇

The person

Among Bergoglio's favourite authors are Friedrich Hoelderlein, Jorge Luis Borges and Fjodor Michailowitsch Dostojewski. He can read the Italian and German books in their original since he speaks both languages fluently. He also loves the cinema whereby he especially treasures the works of Roberto Rosselini, Luigi Zampa, Luchino Visconti and Federico Fellini.

◇

His modesty is not 'put on' as some critics maintain and does not stand in contrast to his decisive, strong and forceful character. Bergoglio is a complex person who, before he became Pope, was also once described as an 'austere Man of God' although he appreciates good and wholesome food. He was also described, amongst other things, as taciturn and media shy which is undoubtedly correct. And yet the world has got to know him as an eloquent speaker who speaks without script and straight from the heart.

◇

A girl from his youth remembered in a TV interview the 15th birthday of Bergoglio's younger sister - it was a party with the hip music of the 50's. The atmosphere was great, only Jorge was quiet and reserved, unwilling to dance. High spirited fun just wasn't up his street and never would be. The only thing he loved was the tango, the melancholic dance of the Argentines. In his youth he was often to be seen in tango bars where he danced to his heart's content.

The tango was to have a repercussion for him years later. The latin word 'tango' (I touch) was spoken by Bergoglio as well as the other 114 Cardinals before the rounds of voting took place in the Conclave. He swore with his hand on the Gospel: "Et ego Jorge Cardinalis Bergoglio spondeo, voveo ac iuro. Sic me Deus adiuvet et haec Sancta Dei Evangelia, quae manu mea tango." (And I, Jorge Cardinal Bergoglio, do so promise, pledge and swear. So help me God and this Holy Gospel which I touch with my hand.) One wonders whether he thought of the tango at that moment and the music to which he had danced in his youth.

◇

The Argentine member of parliament Elisa Carrió said in the press a few days after Bergoglio had been elected Pope that the Holy Father has a heart of steel. She must have meant by this that he, in spite of his apparent mildness and tender gestures towards people in need, has a strength and power of self-assertion which should not be under-estimated. Carrió compared him to St. Francis of Assisi who had not been afraid to approach the Roman leaders bare-footed. And so the tale was spread that Bergoglio would attend his inauguration in sandals. It wasn't quite as bad as this but at least the journalists found it interesting enough to remark on what he would wear on his feet.

◇

In the middle of the 1980's Bergoglio spent some time in Germany. Amongst other things, he intensified his studies at the Philosophy Theologian School of St. Georgen in Frankfurt. His doctorate project which he had begun remained, however, unfinished. Apart from his studies he learned German at the Goethe Institute in Boppard. There in Rheinland Patinate he rented a room with a German couple, Helen and Josef Schmidt. It was all very cosy there, the future Pope often sat on the couch in the living room and listened to the piano playing of his host. The Schmidts say that Bergoglio loved company and was loathe to sit alone in his room. He also preferred to pray in the garden, walking up and down the neatly cut lawn and not wanting to be disturbed. After his return to Argentina they stayed in contact. The Schmidts regularly received airmail letters from South America at Christmas, Easter and birthdays, the addresses always typed on his old typewriter and the letters neatly written with a fountain-pen. So, although they were always informed about what was happening with their former tenant, they never thought that he would one day become Pope.

◇

During his stay in Germany Bergoglio visited Augsburg and made a pilgrimage to the Church of St. Peter Perlach. He was especially impressed with the baroque mercy picture of 'Mary untier of knots'. And he had copies made and took them back to Argentina where the painting of the Swabian Georg Melchior Schmidtner since then enjoys a certain popularity.

◇

Bergoglio brought an original cuckoo clock back with him to Argentina. He was at first delighted with this souvenir from the Black Forest and proudly showed it to all his visitors. Every hour on the hour the bird popped out and sang cuckoo. But slowly the ticking of the clock began to get on his nerves, it disturbed him especially during his time of prayer. Eventually Bergoglio took it down from the wall and gave it to the Jesuit House in Buenos Aires where it apparently still hangs in one of the rooms.

◇

Still a priest, the present Pope taught his nephew and Godson Jorge Vallejos rude words. His sister Maria Elena Bergoglio didn't find this funny at all. One day it led to a highly embarassing situation. Whilst her brother was giving an important sermon her son, on espying his uncle, gave vent to a very rude word which was heard by all and sundry in the church. After the mass Jorge Mario Bergoglio came up to his family and just couldn't stop laughing.

◇

When his nephew was still a baby Bergoglio had dipped his dummy into a glass of whisky. His sense of fun and such escapades were inherited from his father, so his sister says.

The Archbishop

Guillermo Marcó, a very close friend of the Pope, once said that Bergoglio in his middle fifties believed that he had fullfilled his mission in the service of God. At that time he left the capital for Cordoba, a university town, far away from Buenos Aires, to continue his teaching as theologian at its High School. But Bergoglio´s 'second birth' took place in 1998 with his appointment as Metropolitan Archbishop of Buenos Aires. In 2001 he was then appointed Cardinal by Pope John Paul II with the title of cardinal-priest of San Roberto Bellarmino, a church served by Jesuits. When Bergoglio travelled to Rome for the ceremony, he and his sister María Elena visited the village in northern Italy where their father was born. Almost four years later he was shortly before being elected Pope.

◇

The Archbishop used to ride in a public bus to the Favelas, the poorest quarters of Buenos Aires, and walked alone or only accompanied by a single clergyman through streets where not even the police dared to go. He visited these slums, made up of a labyrinth of brick buildings with cor-rugated iron roofs, primitive electricity and con-trolled by the South American mafia, four or five times a year. Bergoglio was not worried or frigh-tened at all, his own safety was not so important for him. His opinion was that the clergy should not lock themselves up in the sacristy but should go out on to the streets to the people. Especially to the poor. Bergoglio set a perfect example. When visiting, he always wore a black cloak and carried a black notice book under his arm. On Maundy Thursday 2012, he knelt down in front of a row of women and children in a church social station and washed their feet.

◇

Deep down he remains conservative even if his behaviour appears rather relaxed and in some cases rather unconventional for a high Catholic clergyman. He christened children for example without asking about the marital status of the mo-ther. On one occasion he christened a mother's seven children even though they were not all from the same father! He afterwards invited ever-ybody for Cola and sausage rolls. The mother of the children thanked him politely and admitted that the generosity of the Bishop had given her a feeling of value and importance. Bergoglio laughed and answered that it wasn't him that had done this but Jesus Christ: "For Him you are especially valuable."

◇

Instead of living in the elegant Bishop's Palace in the suburb of Olivos, Bergoglio chose to stay in a small apartment in Buenos Aires and to cook for himself. Cooking is a real hobby of his - he apparently inherited his talent from his mother. Circumstances forced him to learn cooking and taking care of the house at an early age since his mother, after the birth of her fifth child, was paralysed and had to teach her children to take care of the house and home. Naturally Bergoglio loves Italian food and especially that of the region of his forefathers where beef, partridge and pheasant are special favourites. Most of all he likes roast chicken - but only without the skin! - and accompanied by a glass of wine and for dessert fresh fruit or zabaglione - the famous dish from Piedmont made of eggs, sugar and Muscat wine. He likes to eat alone and refuses invitations to dinner. But with one exception - if he is invited for a meal of 'Bagna Cauda', a sort of Piedmont fondue made up of raw vegetables dipped into a sauce of olive oil, sardines and garlic, he never says no!

Bergoglio and politics

After his ordination to priest in December 1969, Bergoglio quickly rose to the Jesuit-Provincial of Argentina. His term of office also included the time of the Argentine military dictatorship from 1976 to 1983. There are differing opinions of his relationship to the then powers of force. Again and again the story is told of the two monks who were imprisoned under dreadful circumstances in a torture jail and who, after being released, accused Bergoglio of weakness towards the regime. They maintained that the leader of the Jesuits had not stood behind them and protected them. Bergoglio on the other hand explained that a few days before the coup in 1976 he had warned the brothers of the forthcoming danger and had offered them protection in the Jesuit House. One of them, Franz Jalics, has since confirmed that the Holy Father was completely innocent regarding their imprisonment in the 70's. Other church representatives also confirm that there is absolutely no truth in the accusations. On the contrary, Bergoglio helped many dissidents escape the cruelty of the military junta.

◇

In his sermons Bergoglio often denounced the political and social conditions in his country. But he never mentioned the ruling couple, Nestor and Cristina Kirchner, by name but only the growth of corruption and avarice in the booming South American country. The metropole Buenos Aires which is ironically translated with 'Good Air' but suffers more and more from the noise of traffic and the smoke of exhausts is described by Bergoglio as a 'mincing machine' which is consuming the poor. He nevers stops explaining that the power of money has a demon effect leading to corruption, drug dealing and trafficking in human beings - even to the trafficking of children!

◇

His strongest criticism of the Kirchner government is about the marriage of homosexuals which, since 2011, is allowed and accepted in Argentina. Bergoglio refers to the law of nature which appears in the Bible. It deals only with the relationship between man and woman.
Bergoglio admits that there have always been homosexuals: "But never in history have they been granted the same status as married people. In our day and age the legal problems of a marriage of people of the same sex compared to a 'normal' marriage arise again and again. It is a

lessening of values and an anthropological step back (...). Our refusal of a relationship between people of the same sex has no religious but an anthropological basis."

◇

Abortion was also a source of argument. In 2006, Bergoglio publicly opposed an attempt by the Argentine government to legalize some cases of abortion. One can assume that Pope Francis will never budge one millimetre from his standpoint on these two topics.

◇

Bergoglio violently disagrees with the conclusion that celibacy is the reason for sexual abuse in the Church: "If a priest is paedophile he was paedophile before he entered the Church." His attitude to this is quite clear - one may not simply ignore such incidents. Whilst still a bishop a colleague called him and asked for advice in a particular case. Bergoglio told him: "Take away his canon license, don't allow him to preach and begin immediately with the necessary steps to bring him before the Church Tribunal (....). To transfer the

priest somewhere else is pointless. He will always have this problem in his suitcase."

◇

Once Pope, Bergoglio forgot his old feuds. One
of his first actions after being ordained was to in-
vite his old sparring partner Cristina Kirchner to
lunch. She brought him Mate tea from his home-
land and asked for his mediation in the Falkland
conflict. When saying goodbye he pressed a kiss
on the cheek of the heavily made up lady. She is
supposed to have blushed deeply.

◇

Pope Francis
Conclave and Election

He almost became Pope in April 2005.
Cardinal Bergoglio was apparently able to win
forty of the 115 votes. Only by standing down in
favour of the first placed Cardinal Joseph Ratzinger from Germany made the majority vote for
Ratzinger possible.

◇

Before he travelled to the Conclave eight years
later friends and acquaintances collected money
since they could not accept that the Archbishop
of Buenos Aires travels to the Holy City in worn-
out shoes. They bought him a new, black pair. He
accepted them although it was always difficult for
him to accept any sort of present.

◇

Shortly after 7.00 pm on Tuesday the 13th of
March 2013, white smoke rose from the chimney
of the Sistine Chapel. This meant that one name

had been given the necessary two-thirds majority by the 115 Cardinals of the Conclave. Within minutes masses of pilgrimers had streamed to the Via della Concilazione which leads to the Vatican as well as to the narrow streets round about. Hundreds of thousands gathered on St. Peter's Square and called out "Viva Papa".
Bells rang out throughout the city. The bell of St. Peter's was the first to ring out the news. They were moving moments.

◇

Actually, the Gothic Cathedral in Cologne, Germany, was supposed to be the first church worldwide to announce the end of the election in Rome. The Provost, Norbert Feldhoff, had placed three 'spies' on St. Peter's Square whose job it was to call Cologne as soon as the white smoke appeared. But then the mobile networks broke down so that the bells of Cologne cathedral rang out one minute after those of St. Peter's.
At the election of Benedict XVI the Cologne cathedral 'won the race'. The bells of St. Peter's only rang after the name had been announced but Cologne's biggest bell, called "The fat Peter", had already rung as soon as the white smoke appeared.

The Cardinal Protodeacon Jean Louis Tauran, a Frenchman, was the first to appear on the balcony of St. Peter's Basilica and spoke the famous wording: "Annuntio vobis gaudium magnum, habemus Papam!" ("I announce to you with great joy, we have a new Pope!"). The use of these words goes back to the days of the election of Martin V in 1417.

◇

When, as the new Pope at exactly 20.22 hrs Roman time stepped out on to the balcony the crowd at first remained silent. Many seemed to be asking themselves: Who is this man standing up there in a simple white cassock? What can you read in his face? Pope Francis stood there for many minutes, quite still and deeply concentrated. He held himself so stiff and straight, he seemed like a gentle soldier of Jesus. He didn't smile but just looked at the crowd before he greeted them in a quiet voice: "Brothers and Sisters, good evening! As you know, the Conclave was given the task of appointing a new Bishop of Rome. It appears as if my Brothers, the Cardinals, have gone to the end of the world to find one. I thank you for this reception. The diocese of Rome now has its Bishop. Thank you. First of all I would like to pray for our emeritus Bishop Benedict XVI. Let us all pray together that the Lord may bless him and the Mother of God protect him."

The people in Rom, as well as the millions watching on television were touched as he asked for God's blessing before he gave his first blessing as Pope. With this he wanted to give people to understand that he wished to relate his office to God's people and neither desired to stand above Him nor next to Him but to serve Him.

◇

After the proclomation of the new Pope and his speech, the Internet broke down completely as millions wanted to find out more about this unknown stranger from South America via Google.

◇

"May God forgive you for that which you have done" - with this ironic remark, Francis, the new Pope "from the other end of the world" made the Cardinals - most of whom had voted for him - smile. He said this at the end of a short toast after a communal dinner.

The proclomation of the Pope was wildly celebrated in Argentina. In Congress the leader of the
House, Julián Dominguez, interrupted the meeting and simply cried out "We have a new Pope
and he is an Argentine!". On Twitter a slogan
"Los Argentinos Dominan ElMundo" - "the Argentines now rule the world" appeared. This can
hardly be disclaimed since South America is the
continent of the Catholics: In 2010 around 425
490 000 Catholics were living there. 76.8% of Argentines are Catholic!

◇

For the first time since the Syrian Gregor III (from
731 to 741 Pope in Rome) there was a non-Euro-
pean Pope. Jorge Mario Bergoglio is not only the
first South American Pope but also the first Jesuit
sitting on the Holy Chair. This was why some
Cardinals wanted to persuade him to be called
Clemens XV as a reprisal against the Pope who,
as Clemens XIV, wanted to forbid the order of Jesuits in the 18th century. But who thinks at a
time of such celebration of revenge? And did not
Christ teach us how important it is to forgive ?

◇

It is a matter of fact that Ignatius of Loyola (1491-1556) whilst still alive was regarded with some suspicion. The Inquisition suspected him of being a follower of Luther, he was imprisoned, inquisitioned but then released. In 1534 the mystic had a vision and as a result formed the "Society of Jesus" whose members, apart from taking the normal vows on chastity, poverty and obedience towards superiors, committed themselves to absolute recognition of the Pope. The number of Jesuits rose rapidly - when Ignatius died there were already a thousand members - and the Order became an elite group within the Catholic Church. In later centuries the Jesuits were followed again and again, they were accused of plotting and conspiring within the Church. In 1773 the Order was prohibited for almost forty years, a measure taken by the afore mentioned Pope Clemens XIV.

Today there are about 18.000 Jesuits worldwide. Members serve in 112 nations on six continents with the largest number in India and the USA. The headquarters of the society, its General Curia, is in Rome. Jorge Mario Bergoglio became a member of the Jesuits in 1958, he studied theology and philosophy.

"Normally a Jesuit does not seek titles or honours in the Church. But he does not refuse when asked to take up a certain position of responsibility." So we were told by the Province of the German monastic order.

The Holy Father enjoys telling the story of why he spontaneously decided to take the name of Francis:

He was in the Conclave in the Sistine Chapel with 114 other Cardinals under Michaelangelo's painting "Last Judgement". After a number of ballots his name was called out more and more often. Bergoglio, known as something of a joker, when hearing his name always muttered:

"Now it's getting really dangerous for me." When he finally got the two-thirds majority of 77 votes and it was clear that he would become the new Pope, his friend, the Archbishop of Sao Paolo, took him in his arms and whispered: "Don't forget the poor." Bergoglio took this short reminder to heart and he immediately remembered Saint Francis of Assisi and how important his message was for the world of today: "He brought to Christianity an ideal of poverty against the luxury, pride and vanity of the civil and ecclesiastical powers of the time. He changed history." With this snap decision Bergoglio maybe also thought of his father who had died at the age of 51 of a heart problem and whose third Christian name had been Francisco.

◇

The Church has other important members who were also named Francis - Francis of Sales, the imposing mystic and teacher and the missionary Francis Xaver (also a Jesuit) are but two examples. Francis Xaver not only shared the Order with the Pope but also Spanish as mother tongue. In the 16th century he brought the Gospel far away to Japan and China.

◇

There are certain taboos connected with the choice of name for a new Pope. So neither the name of the Saviour Himself nor the names of the twelve Apostles (and especially not that of Saint Peter) nor the first names of the Evangelists can be considered. But none of the 265 Bishops of Rome had ever thought of taking the name of Francis as his official name. When we think of the Middle Ages this seems astonishing since Francis of Assisi was one of the most glowingly admired saints of the roman-catholic church.

◇

Francis of Assisi came from a wealthy cloth trading family and had only one wish: to serve God and to demonstrate this service with a life of abstinence and sacrifice. He once kneeled down in front of Pope Innocence III together with 12 other brothers and asked only to be allowed to be poor. For years he walked through the streets with the sick, the abandoned and the poorest of the poor. In 1219 he joined the Crusade and even prayed with Muslim soldiers. He even brought the word of God to animals, whose language he was supposed to have spoken, and read them passages from the Bible. Many of his fellow-men regarded him as a 'new Christ'. Only two years after his death, Pope Gregor IX, in 1228, canonised him. The new Pope, as a Jesuit, showed remarkable self confidence in adopting the name of Francis.

◇

The speaker of the Vatican, Federico Lombardi, hurried to explain that the figure I. was not to be used after the name Francis until a second Pope took this name too. Part of the media had already called him 'Francis the First'. This was wrong - Francis is simply Francis.

◇

His new coat of arms is similar to the previous coat of arms of the Archbishop only that the stars and the nard blooms are golden instead of silver. The blue shield shows the emblem of the "Society of Jesus" which is made up of a golden sun with the red Christian monogramm IHS (a monogram of the Holy Name of Jesus), with a red cross surmounting the H and three black nails below the H. Below the Jesuit emblem is on the left an eight-pointed star, which is a long-standing symbol of the Blessed Virgin Mary, and on the right a nard flower symbolizing Saint Joseph. Francis' motto remains 'Miserando atque eligende' (Latin for: by having mercy and by choosing). This saying goes back to the anglo-saxon monk Beda Venerabilis (673-735) and is part of a bible text in which Jesus chose Matthew as an apostle. We hear from the Vatican that when Jorge Mario Bergoglio, then 17, decided to become a priest this text played a decisive role for him.

◇

Maria Elena Bergoglio is the only one of the Pope's sisters still alive. She lives with her family in Ituzaurigo, a suburb of Buenos Aires, and telephones regularly with her eleven years older brother.

On the Saturday after the papal election he tele-
phoned her but only for a few minutes. The Pope
asked her to tell the whole family that he was
fine, that he couldn't call each of them individual-
ly and that he couldn't talk for long since he wanted to avoid a high telephone bill for the Vatican.
He commented on his election by saying that
things had just turned out that way -
"I couldn't say no."

◇

Maria Elena, as well as having feelings of happiness and pride at being the sister of the Holy Father, was also worried about him. Many years
previously she had met Pope John Paul II in
Rome when her brother became Cardinal. "I knelt
down, kissed his ring and saw much love in his
eyes. But also a great loneliness. I can see much
love in the eyes of my brother but I do hope that
he will not feel lonely."

◇

Maria Elena's son Jorge Vallejos followed the
Pope election on the Internet. When he realised
that his uncle had been elected Pope he was at
first shocked and had to sit down. Jorge admitted

that he had mixed feelings - on the one hand he was happy for his uncle but on the other he was already missing him very much.

◇

His tendency to humility soon became legendary and was talked about everywhere. Apparently Pope Francis, immediately after the election, told his Master of Ceremonies, Monsignore Guido Marini, quite clearly that he would not wear the red velvet mozzetta with white ermine fur. "You wear it!", he suggested. And with the very next sentence Bergoglio emphasised that a demonstration of simplicity would be a basic part of his Pontifax: "The carnival is over," he said.
On that Wednesday evening he walked alone and incognito through the narrow streets around the Vatican. The new Pope didn't use the state limousine with the number plate 'Vatican 1' either but rode back to his lodgings with the Cardinals in a minibus. At 8 am next day he went to his hotel in the Via della Scrofa to pick up his luggage and to pay his bill
- out of his own pocket of course.

◇

On the same day he visited Cardinal Jorge Maria
Mejía in hospital and chatted
with patients and staff.
Later that day the Holy Father felt the need to
pray to the Mother of God. Many Romans knew
where he would go - to the Basilica 'Santa Maria
Maggiore' on the Esquilins Hill. This 5th century
church is famous for its early Christian mosaics
but above all there is the 'Maria Salus Populi Ro-
mani' (Protectress of the Roman People), a By-
zantine icon of the Madonna and Child which has
historically been the most important Marian icon
in Rome.
And the Pope is first and foremost the Bishop of
Rome. In the Basilica he knelt before the picture
of the Virgin Mary and prayed. He prayed for 10
minutes and then placed flowers on the altar.
Afterwards he spent some time in another
chapel, in which Ignatius of Loyola, the founder
of the Order of Jesuits, celebrated his
first Christmas Mass.

◇

On the Thursday Bergoglio celebrated his first
Mass in the Sistine Chapel at a so-called 'people's altar' where the front and back were con-
structed of cheap plywood. Pope John Paul II
had had this made but his successor Benedict

XVI had it removed. The Pontifax from Bavaria held the Mass from the original high altar at the head end of the chapel facing God. Francis, on the other hand, faced his Cardinals once more during Mass.

With this he not only demonstrated a change of direction but also a new world outlook!

◇

The first German words which he spoke with a slight Spanish accent were a quote from the birthday poem from Friedrich Hoelderlein to his grandmother: 'Old age is quiet and pious'. This happened at his first audience for his Cardinals in the Sala Clementina in the Apostolic Palace on the Friday, two days after his election. The Pope spoke, in view of the older ages of the Cardinals, of the importance of old age as the 'Seat of Wisdom'. This wisdom must be passed on to the younger generation.

◇

"Cari fratelli - Forza!" - "Dear Brothers - off you go!" With an enthusiastic smile on his face and with high-spirited gestures he called out to the Cardinals on Friday morning in the Apostle Palace. He summoned them to new dynamism in the spreading of the Word of God and Christianity.

◇

On Sunday the 17th of March Pope Francis appeared punctually at 12 noon at the window of his new office to pray the 'Angelus' for the first time as Pope. He recited the 'Ave Maria' in Latin and spontaneous applause broke out again and again. After the Apostolic Blessing he had a further surprise up his sleeve: Instead of the usual greeting in all languages he simply said "Buon pranzo" - "Enjoy your lunch". A little later he sent the following message via Twitter @Pontifax: "Dear Friends, I thank you from the bottom of my heart and simply ask you to continue to pray for me."

◇

In the mean time he has more than two million followers on Twitter. He had won the hearts of the believers very quickly. Jorge Mario Bergoglio is probably the first Pope to have his own Facebook page - he had set it up way before his election:

www.facebook.com/JorgeMarioBergoglio. The number of users who like it rises from hour to hour.

◇

With such a fanatic football fan as the Pope it didn't last long before the first football jokes were making the rounds: the sports paper "Olé" mentioned in their online edition for instance the legendary 'handball' of Diego Maradona in the semi-final of the World Cup in 1986. Above a photo of the Pope standing on his balcony and waving to his followers the paper titled: "La Mano de Dios" - "The Hand of God".

◇

In his first week in office Pope Francis had received the Superior General of the Jesuits, Adolfo Nicolás, in the Vatican guesthouse. And after greeting him with jesuitical embrace Pope Francis made it quite clear that he did not want to be adressed as 'Your Holiness' or 'Holy Father'. He asked Nicolas to treat him as he would treat any other Jesuit and to speak to him on first-name terms.

Francis is a real fright for his bodyguards since he always seeks the nearness of the people even up to wanting to touch them and be touched. On the first Sunday after his election he was in amongst the crowd in front of the entrance to the Vatican church Sant'Anna die Palafrenieri. He shook hands and didn't once try to avoid anybody. Nobody had ever before searched the crowd for weapons and the Pope just wouldn't hear of it. "Why? There is absolutely no reason," he said.

The chief of the bodyguards, Domenico Giani, had no choice but to leave things as they were and to look on with a really sour face.

◇

Five days after the papal election the phone rang in the house of family Del Regno in Buenos Aires. Son Daniel answered and first of all believed that one of his friends was playing a trick on him. Somebody had just said on the phone: "Hello Daniel, here is Cardinal Jorge". It turned out that it really was the Pope from Rome who merely wanted to cancel his newspaper subscription. Daniel's father, Luis Del Regno, is the owner of a kiosk where the former Cardinal subscribed to his daily newspaper. On workdays a kiosk employee would bring the newspaper to the Cardinal's

home but on Sundays Bergoglio used to walk to
the kiosk, collect his newspaper and have
a little chat with Luis Del Regno.

Bergoglio had never believed, when leaving
Buenos Aires at the beginning of March, that he
might not be back for some time. At that time he
had answered Del Regno's question about what
he thought of his chances with the remark:
"That's rather a hot potato. I'll be back in twenty
days, just keep on delivering
the newspaper as usual."

◇

The doorman Andreas was so confused when he
heard the Pope personally on the telephone asking to be connected with the Superior General
of the Jesuits, Father Adolfo Nicolás, that it needed a few words from the Pope to calm him
down. He asked Andreas for his name and asked
after his good health. Andreas admitted that he
was most confused and Francis replied that he
could well understand this and waited patiently
for Andreas to connect him.

◇

Francis also called his former archdiocese in Buenos Aires personally. He was asked who was speaking. He simply said: "Father George."
"Your Holiness?" was the next question.
"Oh come on, Father George is on the line."
He caused much confusion at his dentists when he rang up personally from Rome to cancel his next appointment!

◇

The Germans still can maintain just a little that 'We are the Pope' (which was the headline of Germany's biggest tabloid paper – the BILD Zeitung – in 2005 when Joseph Ratzinger became Pope).
The name Bergoglio originates from German. The well known name researcher Prof. Juergen Udolph from Leipzig pointed out that the name Bergoglio comes from the old christian name Beriko for 'bear' i.e. from the German word 'Berg' which means mountain.
And to have the word 'mountain' in your secular name has a special meaning for a present day Pope: after all Jesus said to Simon Peter (Matthew 16,18): "And I say also unto thee, that thou art Peter, and upon this rock I will build my church, and the gates of hell shall not prevail against it."

Inauguration

The whole world seems to be mad about Pope Francis. 132 government delegates came to Rome on the 19th of March 2013 for his inauguration (the largest delegation came from Germany and was led by Chancellor Angela Merkel). Among the 132 were 33 heads of state, twelve prime ministers and six reigning monarchs. After Mass everyone was allowed to shake hands with the new Pope. Argentina's president Cristina Kirchner was the first to congratulate him since he is an Argentine. Giorgio Napolitano, Italy's state president, and the ruling minister president, Mario Monti, followed. All congratulations were made in record time, everyone had exactly 30 seconds and this was controlled by stopwatch!

◇

About half an hour before the Mass, Francis toured the square in the popemobile to greet the crowds. He stopped and left the popemobile once to kiss a disabled man.

◇

The Pope's meeting with Simbabwe's long time dictator, Robert Mugabe, was followed with curiosity by the general public. Mugabe is not allowed to enter EU countries but he may visit the Vatican. The Pope behaved most diplomatically and exchanged a few words with Mugabe as he did with the other members of the delegation.

◇

Politically speaking, the first visit of a Greek Orthodox Patriarch, Barthomolaios from Istanbul, to an inauguration of a Pope since the splitting of the Church in 1054, caused a sensation. Until then, people in his position had at the most visited the Vatican for a funeral. The embrace between the Pope and Barthomolaios was regarded as an important sign for the unity of the Church. Both arranged a journey to Jerusalem together. The Princes of the church thus want to intensify and improve relations between their churches.

◇

Which shoes does the Pope wear? This somewhat profane question interests the world tremendously.

Francis' predecessor Benedict XVI always wore the fine red mocassins. But does this fine footwear suit the new Pope? No, of course not, and so on the 19th of March the Holy Father wore simple black shoes with laces. And he insisted on tying them himself!

◇

The Pontifax prefers silver and silvercoloured metals to the more expensive and more precious gold. For example: As Piscatory Ring – the Fisherman's ring which symbolises the Pope as successor to Saint Peter who was a fisherman – Francis recycled a gilded silver ring from the time of Paul VI and the second
Vatican Council.
And he didn't want to forfeit his iron cross for the Pope's golden cross.
Has this preference maybe a connection to his place of birth? Argentina is derived from the latin word for silver - argentum - and points to the fact that the Spanish invaders were hoping to find lots of this in the newly conquered continent.

◇

The Holy Mass at the inauguration was celebrated on St. Peter's Square by 180 Cardinals and Bishops. The readings were read in Spanish and English. The Gospel was sung by a deacon in Greek underlining the close relationship to the eastern churches. Intercessions were given in Russian, Arabic and Mandarin. There were more than 300.000 people present. The highspot of the ceremony: under the eyes of the crowned heads, Francis was equipped with the signia of his office - the Piscatory Ring and the Pallium, a lamb's wool shawl. On this occasion Francis did not want to see any supporters from Argentina. He felt that it was just too much that so many people would make such a long trip just to see him on his big day. He had already told the Bishops and other believers to stay at home and give the so saved money to people who really needed it. But the Argentines in their euphory were not to be stopped from travelling to Rome. And the football fans especially were not to be kept from staying away - they mounted a photograph of their Pope on to a huge flag of their first division team San Lorenzo and waved it again and again for the benefit of their most famous fan.

◇

Always very close to the Pontifax is the good-loo-
king German Archbishop Georg Gaenswein -
also known as the 'Vatican's George Clooney'.
He is the Prefect of the Papal Household as well
as being the personal secretary of the pope-eme-
ritus, Benedict XVI. He doesn't seem to mind -
on the contrary he loves - the unpretentious man-
ner of his new 'boss'. One of his first official actions was to help Francis out of a fix: the door to
the Pope's flat wouldn't open the first time he
wanted to enter. Gaenswein knew of this problem
and was able to open the door immediately without difficulty. He then conducted the Pope with
a group of Cardinals from room to room.

◇

The Holy Father decided to use only a few rooms
of the Apostolic Palace. "There is enough room
here for 300," he was quoted as saying after he
had inspected the building. He wanted to stay in
the Vatican's guesthouse 'Domus Sanctae Mar-
tae' (Saint Martha's House) until his furniture and
private belongings arrived. At least he had exchanged the small room which he was given to
use at the time of the proclamation for a three-
roomed flat (Suite 201) where he was able to re-
ceive official visitors. He only used the large Pope's flat to step out on to the balcony to give his
Angelus prayer. Apart from this he uses the libra-

ry in the Pope's palace to work in. Pope Francis is the first pope not to live in the papal apartment on the third floor of the Apostolic Palace since Pope Pius X first moved into it in 1903.

◇

In 'Saint Martha's House' he got on very well with the employees and was very happy to be staying there. He moved completely uncomplicated between the other guests and sat in the dining room wherever there was a seat available. He celebrated mass on a Friday morning in the small church belonging to the guesthouse together with the other guests. The house was completely full until Easter since fifteen Cardinals wanted to stay on in Rome until the end of Lent. "Pope Francis cannot stay on in the guesthouse because of problems regarding his security," was heard from the Vatican at the beginning. But who knows? The house is used all the time as a hotel by bishops, nuns and advisors to the Vatican.

◇

When the Pope sees new people in the Vatican guesthouse he always approaches them and asks who they are and where they come from. He once met the second youngest Cardinal in the Catholic Church, Louis Antonio Tagle, the Archbishop of Manila who, at 55, looked extremely young. On top of which he was very leisurely dressed so that the Pope, thinking he was a seminary student, simply said to him: "Good morning young man." When the Cardinal explained who he was and how ashamed he was not to be wearing his clergy apparel, the Pope simply replied: "Oh, you look great, I like it."

◊

On Saturday a special and unique meeting in the 2.000 year history of the Catholic Church took place in the Pope's summer residence Castel Gandolfo, thirty kilometres south of Rome. The new Pope visited the old one, the newly elected Pope the emerite. Benedict XVI was waiting on the helicopter landing ground as Francis arrived at noon. They prayed in the Castel church before retiring to the library for a 45 minute talk between themselves. The former Pope offered his successor the place of honour who then answered that they were both brothers and that they should kneel down together at the same bench.

They were both dressed in white - caps and sou-
tanes were white and even their hair matched!
Bendict XVI used a walking stick but appeared to
be robust and was very moved. They often held
each other's hands and Benedict gave Francis a
present of an icon - the 'Madonna of Humility'.
On Palm Sunday the Pope reminded everyone
not to let themselves be discouraged by difficul-
ties. "Our happiness does not depend on material things but on our love of Jesus. With Him we
are never alone, not even at those difficult times
when we feel that the problems are insurmounta-
ble. It is necessary to retain a 'young heart' in old
age. He who lives in Jesus Christ will never grow
old." On leaving St. Peter's Square some believers called out his name. Pope Francis had the
car stopped, stepped out and embraced and kissed the people.

www.frommverlag.de